*Bon App*

# GATEAUX

## FLANS AND CAKES

# Foreword

This little book contains a variety of recipes for fresh cream cakes, fruit flans, and party gateaux - as well as several ideas which may be new to you.

Do be careful to follow one type of measure throughout the recipe. The three measurements given are Metric, Imperial and American (cups). Where American ingredients differ from English, the American name has been put in brackets.

All recipes are for four people unless otherwise stated.

Bon Appétit.

# Black forest cherry gateau

## Ingredients

For the mixture:
*4 eggs*
*4x15ml/4tbs/5tbs lukewarm*
*water*
*100g/4oz/ ¾lb castor sugar*
*(fine granulated)*
*3x5ml/3tsp/3tsp baking powder*
*1x5ml/1tsp/1tsp vanilla essence*
*(extract)*
*100g/4oz/¼lb plain flour*
*(all purpose)*
*100g/4oz/¼lb cornflour*
*(cornstarch)*

For the filling:
*750ml/1¾pts/3 cups double*
*cream (heavy cream)*
*275g/10oz/10oz plain dark*
*chocolate*
*500g/1lb/1lb stoned Morello*
*cherries out of a jar*
*40g/1½oz/3tbs cornflour*
*(cornstarch)*
*1x15ml/1tbs/2tbs castor sugar*
*(fine granulated)*
*2x15ml/2tbs/3tbs Kirsch*
*3x15ml/3tbs/4tbs redcurrant*
*jelly*

Garnish:
*Morello cherries (optional)*


**Method**

Preheat oven to 190°C/375°F/Gas 5.
1   To make the mixture: Separate the egg yolks and whites.
    Beat the yolks with the lukewarm water until frothy.
    Add sugar a little at a time with the vanilla.
    Beat until the mixture is creamy.
2   Whisk the egg whites until they are stiff. Gradually whisk in
    the rest of the sugar.
3   Fold the yolk mixture through the egg whites.
4   Sift the flour, cornflour and baking powder together and fold
    through the mixture.
5   Pour into a greased-spring-release cake tin, lined with greased
    greaseproof paper. Cook in preheated oven for 25 - 35 minutes.
6   To make the filling: Bring cream and chocolate to the boil,
    slowly stirring all the while. Boil briefly then pour into a bowl
    and leave to cool overnight.
7   Drain the cherries. Measure 250ml/8fl oz/1 cup cherry juice, (if
    necessary extend with water). Blend 4x15ml/4tbs/5tbs
    cornflour. Bring the rest of the cherry juice to the boil.
    Remove the juice from the heat and pour in the cornflour
    mixture, stirring constantly. Bring back to the boil briefly. Stir
    in the cherries and flavour with sugar and Kirsch. Leave the
    filling to cool.
8   Cut the cake twice horizontally to make 3 layers of cake.
9   Stir the redcurrant jelly together with a·little lukewarm water to
    make a smooth mixture. Spread the jelly mixture on to the
    bottom layer of cake. Then put on the middle layer and spread
    this with the cherry filling mixture.
10  Beat the chocolate cream until it is stiff.
    Spread 5x15ml/5tbs/6tbs of chocolate cream over the cooled
    cherry mixture. Cover with the third layer of cake. Use the
    remaining chocolate cream to cover the sides and top of the
    cake. The cake can be decorated with cherries.

# Hazelnut cream cake

(illustrated pages 8-9)

## Ingredients

For the mixture:
*3 eggs*
*100g/4oz/ ¼lb castor sugar*
*(fine granulated)*
*1x5ml/1tsp/1tsp vanilla essence*
*(extract)*
*75g/3oz/6tbs flour*
*salt*
*25g/1oz/2tbs cornflour*
*(cornstarch)*
*coffee liqueur*

For the filling:
*750ml/1¼pts/3 cups double*
*cream (heavy cream)*
*175g/6oz/6oz toasted hazelnuts,*
*ground*
*5x15ml/5tbs/6tbs cold milk*

Garnish:
*grated nuts and whole hazelnuts*

## Method

Preheat oven to 180°C/350°F/Gas 4.
1   To make the mixture: Separate the eggs and whisk the whites until they are stiff. Beat in the sugar and vanilla a spoonful at a time. Beat in the yolks one by one. Add the flour with a pinch of salt.
2   Sieve the cornflour and fold into the mixture carefully but thoroughly.
3   Pour the mixture into a greased cake tin lined with greased greaseproof paper (approx 23cm/9''). Cook in preheated oven for 25-35 minutes.
    When the cake has cooled, cut through once horizontally and sprinkle the two layers with coffee liqueur.
4   To make the filling: Beat the cream until stiff, fill a piping bag with 3x15ml/3tbs/4tbs of the cream for garnishing.
5   Fold the ground hazelnuts into the rest of the cream.
6   Spread ⅓ of the hazelnut cream on the bottom layer of cake. Place the other layer of cake on top. Spread the top layer of cake evenly with the rest of the cream.
7   Decorate the top of the cake with the cream in the piping bag. Garnish with the grated nuts and whole hazelnuts.
    Chill the cake until firm. (Do not leave in the refrigerator).

# Mocha ring

## Ingredients

For the mixture:
*2 eggs*
*3x15ml/3tbs/4tbs warm water*
*100g/4oz/ ¼lb castor sugar*
*(fine granulated)*
*1x5ml/1tsp/1tsp vanilla*
*essence (extract)*
*75g/3oz/6tbs plain flour*
*(all purpose)*
*50g/2oz/4tbs cornflour*
*(cornstarch)*
*1x5ml/1tsp/1tsp baking powder*

For the filling:
*500ml/18fl oz/2 ¼cups double*
*cream (heavy cream), chilled*
*2x5ml/2tsp/2tsp instant coffee*

Garnish:
*100g/4oz/ ¼lb chocolate flakes*
*chocolate dots*
*glacé cherries*

## Method

Preheat oven to 180°C/350°F/Gas 4.
1   To make mixture: Separate the eggs. Stir the yolks together
    with the warm water until it is frothy. Gradually add ⅔ of the
    sugar and vanilla. Beat until the mixture is thick and mousse-
    like. Whisk the whites until stiff and whip in the rest of the
    sugar. Fold the yolk mixture into the whites.
2   Mix the flour, cornflour and baking powder. Sieve and fold
    into the mixture (do not stir). Pour into a greased ring-shaped
    cake tin (23cm/9"). Bake in a preheated oven until well risen
    and golden - about 30 minutes.
3   To make the filling: Beat the chilled cream for ½ minute.
    Add the instant coffee to the cream and continue whipping
    until it is completely stiff.
4   Cut the cake through twice horizontally and spread with mocha
    cream. Put some of the cream aside for garnishing.
5   Decorate the cake with the remaining cream and garnish with
    chocolate flakes, chocolate dots and glacé cherries.

# Strawberry cream cake

## Ingredients

For the mixture:
*2 eggs*
*3x15ml/3tbs/4tbs warm water*
*100g/4oz/¼lb castor sugar*
*(fine granulated)*
*1x5ml/1tsp/1tsp/baking*
*powder*
*1x5ml/1tsp/1tsp vanilla essence*
*(extract)*
*75g/3oz/6tbs plain flour*
*(all purpose)*
*50g/2oz/4tbs cornflour*
*(cornstarch)*

For the filling and icing
(frosting):
*250ml/8fl oz/1 cup*
*confectioners custard*
*(pastry cream)*
*500g/1lb/1lb strawberries*
*500ml/18fl oz/2 ¼ cups double*
*cream (heavy cream)*
*50g/2oz/4tbs icing sugar*
*(confectioners)*
*1x5ml/1tsp/1tsp vanilla essence*
*(extract)*

Decoration:
*about 6 strawberries*

## Method

Preheat oven to 180°C/350°F/Gas 4.

1  To make the mixture: Separate the eggs. Stir yolks with warm water until frothy. Gradually add ⅔ of the sugar with the vanilla. Beat until the mixture is creamy and mousse-like. Beat the whites until they are stiff. Gradually beat in the rest of the sugar. Fold the yolk mixture into the whites.

2  Sift together the flour, cornflour and baking powder and fold into the mixture (do not stir). Pour into a greased spring-release cake tin (25cm/10") lined with greased greaseproof paper. Bake until golden, 20-30 minutes. Leave the cake to cool completely.

3  To make the filling and icing (frosting): Wash, hull and drain the strawberries. Whip the cream and vanilla for half a minute. Sieve the icing sugar into the cream and continue to beat until stiff.

4   Cut the cake through once horizontally. Spread the bottom layer with confectioners custard and lay strawberries on top. Spread ⅓ of the cream evenly over the strawberries. Place the second layer on top and press gently. Spread the sides and top of the cake smoothly with the cream. Use the remaining cream for piping on the top and decorate with halved strawberries.

# Levantine cake

## Ingredients

For the mixture:
*175g/6oz/6oz unsalted butter*
*175g/6oz/6oz castor sugar*
*(fine granulated)*
*3 eggs*
*salt*
*1x5ml/1tsp/1tsp vanilla*
*essence (extract)*
*175g/6oz/6oz plain flour*
*(all purpose)*
*2x5ml/2tsp/2tsp baking powder*

For the filling and topping:
*500ml/18fl oz/2¼ cups double*
*cream (heavy cream)*
*2x15ml/2tbs/3tbs icing sugar*
*(confectioners)*
*1x5ml/1tsp/1tsp vanilla essence*
*100g/4oz/¼lb ground toasted*
*hazelnuts*

Decoration:
*whole toasted hazelnuts*

## Method

Preheat oven to 180°C/350°F/Gas 4.

1  To make the mixture: Cream the butter and sugar until light
and fluffy. Beat in the eggs one by one. Add salt and vanilla.

2  Sift the flour and baking powder together and fold gradually
into the egg mixture. (Do not stir.) Pour into a greased spring-
release cake tin (25cm/10") lined with greased greaseproof
paper. Bake in a preheated oven for approximately 45 minutes.
Leave the cake to cool completely. Cut through once
horizontally.

3  To make the filling and topping: Beat the chilled cream for half
a minute with the vanilla then add the sifted icing sugar and
whip until stiff. Put a quarter of the cream into a piping bag.

4  (Put aside 25g/1oz/2tbs of ground hazelnuts). Stir the
remaining hazelnuts into the cream. Spread the bottom layer of
cake with the hazelnut cream. Lay the other layer on top.
Spread the sides and top of the cake with some of the cream
from the piping bag. Sprinkle the sides of the cake with the
remaining ground hazelnuts.

5  Decorate with the rest of the cream and garnish with whole
hazelnuts.

# Chocolate cake with Kirsch

**Ingredients**

For the mixture:
*100g/4oz/ ¼lb butter or soft margarine*
*100g/4oz/ ¼lb castor sugar*
*(fine granulated)*
*1x5ml/1tsp/1tsp vanilla essence*
*(extract)*
*2x5ml/2tsp/2tsp baking powder*
*15g/ ½ oz/1tbs cocoa*
*3x15ml/3tbs/4tbs milk*
*2 eggs, beaten*
*salt*
*150g/5oz/5oz plain flour*
*(all purpose)*

For the filling and topping:
*500g/1lb/1lb stoned Morello*
*cherries from a jar*
*25g/1oz/2tbs castor sugar*
*(fine granulated)*
*40g/1½oz/3tbs cornflour*
*(cornstarch)*
*3x15ml/3tbs/4tbs Kirsch*
*500ml/18fl oz/2 ¼ cups double*
*cream (heavy cream)*
*1x5ml/1tsp/1tsp vanilla essence*
*(extract)*
*75g/3oz/3oz plain dark chocolate*

**Method**

Preheat oven to 180°C/350°F/Gas 4.
1   To make the mixture: Cream the butter and sugar until light and fluffy. Gradually beat in the vanilla, eggs and a pinch of salt.
2   Sift together the flour, baking powder and cocoa. Fold into the egg mixture, together with milk. Pour the mixture into a

greased and lined square cake tin (20cm/8''). Bake for approximately 25 minutes.

3   To make the filling and topping: Drain the cherries and reserve the juice. Measure out 250ml/8fl oz/1 cup cherry juice (extend juice with water if necessary). Blend cornflour with 4x15ml/4tbs/5tbs juice. Bring the rest to the boil, remove and stir in the blended cornflour, bring back to the boil then stir in the cherries (retaining 16 cherries for garnishing). Cool.

4   Stir sugar and Kirsch into the cherry mixture and cover the cake with it. Whip the cream with vanilla until stiff. Put ⅓ of the cream into a piping bag with a large rose nozzle.

5   Break the chocolate into small pieces and put in a bowl over boiling water. Stir until it is melted into a smooth mixture.

6   Fold the lukewarm chocolate carefully into the rest of the cream and spread evenly over the cherry mixture.

7   Pipe a lattice of whipped cream over the top, a rosette in the centre of the squares, and top with cherries.

# Chocolate cream cake

## Ingredients

For the mixture:
2 eggs
3x15ml/3tbs/4tbs warm water
100g/4oz/¼lb castor sugar
(fine granulated)
1x5ml/1tsp/1tsp vanilla essence
(extract)
75g/3 oz/6tbs plain flour
(all purpose)
50g/2oz/4tbs cornflour
(cornstarch)
1x5ml/1tsp/1tsp baking powder

For the filling:
750ml/1¼pts/3 cups double
cream (heavy cream)
100g/4oz/¼lb icing sugar,
sifted (confectioners)
1x5ml/1tsp/1tsp vanilla
essence (extract)
25g/1oz/2tbs cocoa

For the icing (frosting):
100g/4oz/¼lb chocolate
1x15ml/1tbs/1tbs butter

Garnish:
Chocolate flakes

## Method

Preheat oven to 180°C/350°F/Gas 4.
1  To make the mixture: Separate the eggs. Stir the yolks and warm water until frothy. Gradually add ⅔ of the sugar and vanilla. Beat until the mixture is creamy and mousse-like. Whip the whites until stiff. Beat in the rest of the sugar. Fold the yolk mixture into the whites.
2  Sift together the flour, cornflour and baking powder. Fold into the mixture (do not stir). Pour into a greased and lined spring-release cake tin (23cm/9") and bake for 23-35 minutes.
3  Leave the cake to cool and then cut through once horizontally.
4  To make the icing (frosting): Stir the chocolate and butter in a bowl over a saucepan of hot water, until it has melted into a smooth mixture. Spread evenly over the top layer of cake.
5  To make the filling: Whip the cream with the icing sugar and vanilla until it is stiff. Put 3x15ml/3tbs/4tbs of cream into a piping bag with a rose nozzle. Sift cocoa and mix into the rest of the cream.

6   Spread a generous ⅔ portion of the cream over the bottom layer of cake.
7   Cut the iced top layer into 12 equal portions. Put these on top of the bottom layer and press down lightly. Spread the sides of the cake with the rest of the cream and then sprinkle with cocoa.
8   Use the cream in the piping bag to decorate the top of the cake and garnish with chocolate flakes.

# Heavenly cake

## Ingredients

For the mixture:
*225g/8oz/½lb butter or soft
margarine
225g/8oz/½lb castor sugar
(fine granulated)
2x5ml/2tsp/2tsp vanilla essence
(extract)
4 eggs
100/4oz/¼lb flaked almonds
salt
225g/8 oz/½lb plain flour
(all purpose)
2x5ml/2tsp/2tsp baking powder
1x5ml/1tsp/1tsp ground
cinnamon*

For the filling:
*500g/1lb/1lb redcurrants
100g/4oz/¼lb icing sugar
(confectioners)
500ml/18fl oz/2¼cups double
cream (heavy cream) chilled*

## Method

Preheat oven to 180°C/350°F/Gas 4.

1   To make the mixture: Separate the eggs. Cream the butter and gradually beat in 200g/7 oz/7 oz sugar, 1x5ml/1tsp/1tsp vanilla, egg yolks and a pinch of salt.

2   Sift together the flour and baking powder, fold into the egg mixture. Beat the whites until stiff. Use the greased bases of 4 spring-release cake tins (23 cm/9"). The sides will not be required. On each base spread 2x15ml/2tbs/3tbs of the cake mixture. The mixture should not be too thinly spread at the sides as this will make the cake too dark.

3   Spread ¼ of the beaten egg white over each layer of the cake mixture.

4   Mix 25g/1oz/2tbs sugar with 1x5ml/1tsp/1tsp vanilla and cinnamon. Take a ¼ of this mixture and ¼ of the almonds and sprinkle over each of the 4 layers of cake mixture.

5   Loosen the cake layers from the tins immediately after removing from the oven.

6   To make the filling: Rinse and string the redcurrants.

Sprinkle with icing sugar.
7 Take the cream and whip until stiff, fold in the redcurrants.
8 Spread each layer with the cream and sandwich them together
to make a layer cake. The top layer should consist of cake.

# Caracas cake

## Ingredients

For the mixture:
4 eggs
100g/4oz/¼lb marzipan or
almond paste, softened
100g/4oz/¼lb castor sugar
(fine granulated)
1x5ml/1tsp/1tsp vanilla essence
(extract)
pinch salt
pinch ground cinnamon
100g/4oz/¼lb plain flour
(all purpose)

2x5ml/2tsp/2tsp baking powder
75g/3oz/6tbs nougat, crushed
50g/2oz/4tbs melted butter or
margarine

For the filling and icing
(frosting):
100g/4oz/¼lb plain dark
chocolate
500ml/18fl oz/2 ¼ cups double
cream (heavy cream)
chocolate squares

## Method

Preheat the oven to 180°C/350°F/Gas 4.
1   To make the mixture: Separate the eggs. Mix the yolks with the
    marzipan and whisk with an electric mixer at the maximum
    speed until it is frothy. Gradually add half the sugar, vanilla,
    salt and cinnamon. Beat until the mixture is creamy. Whip
    whites until stiff. Beat in remaining sugar a little at a time.
    Fold the yolk mixture into the whites.
2   Sift together the flour and baking powder and fold in carefully
    (do not stir). Fold in nougat and melted butter or magarine.
    Pour the mixture into a greased and lined spring-release cake
    tin (23cm/9'') and bake for 25-30 minutes.
3   When the cake is cool, cut it through once horizontally.
4   To make the filling and icing (frosting): Break up the chocolate
    and put it into a bowl over a pan of hot water.
    Stir until it is a smooth mixture. Cool slightly.
5   Whip the cream until it is stiff. Stir in the chocolate mixture.
6   Fill a piping bag fitted with a rose nozzle, with
    4x15ml/4tbs/5tbs chocolate cream. Spread ⅔ of the chocolate
    cream on the bottom layer of cake. Place the other layer on
    top. Spread the sides and top of the cake evenly with the
    remaining chocolate cream.
7   Pipe the top decoratively and garnish with chocolate squares.

# Lemon chocolate cream cake

## Ingredients

For the mixture:
*275g/10oz/10oz plain flour
(all purpose)
2x5ml/2tsp/2tsp baking powder
15g/ ½oz/1tbs cocoa
175g/6oz/6oz castor sugar
(fine granulated)
1x5ml/1tsp/1tsp vanilla essence
(extract)
1 egg
175g cold butter or firm
margarine
175g/6oz/6oz ground hazelnuts*

For the filling:
*3x5ml/3tsp/4tsp gelatine
powder
3x15ml/3tbs/4tbs cold water
1 lemon
5 sugar lumps
750ml/1¼pts/3 cups double
cream (heavy cream)
7x15ml/7tbs/8tbs lemon juice
150g/5oz/5oz icing sugar
(confectioners)*
For the icing (frosting):
*50g/2oz/4tbs chocolate
15g/½oz/1tbs butter*

## Method

Preheat oven to 180°C/350°F/Gas 4.

1 To make the mixture: Sift the flour, baking powder and cocoa on to a pastry board and make a hollow in the middle of the mixture. Put the sugar, vanilla and egg into the centre, work some of the flour into the mixture until it becomes a thick paste. Cut the cold butter or margarine into pieces and add to the mixture. Add the hazelnuts. Working outwards from the centre, quickly knead all the ingredients into a smooth dough and chill until firm.

2 Roll out the dough and divide it into quarters. Spread each piece of the mixture on to the greased bases of 4 spring-release cake tins (23cm/9''). The sides will not be required. Bake until they are golden, 10-15 minutes.

3 Remove cake from the tins directly after baking. Cut one of the cake layers into 16 pieces. Leave to cool.

4 To make the icing (frosting): Break the chocolate into small pieces and stir together with butter in a bowl over a pan of hot water, until it becomes smooth.

5   Spread the chocolate icing evenly on one side of each of the 16 pieces of cake.
6   To make the filling: Put gelatine powder in a pan with cold water. Soak for 10 minutes. Rinse the lemon, dry it and rub the rind with the sugar lumps to extract the oil. Heat the soaked gelatine with the sugar lumps, stirring until dissolved. Add the lemon juice.
7   Whip the cream until it is almost stiff. Pour in the lukewarm gelatine solution, carry on whipping until it is completely stiff. Sift the icing sugar and fold carefully into the cream.
8   Pipe 16 rosettes of cream on to one layer of cake. Spread or pipe a layer of cream on to the top of the two remaining layers. Sandwich them together and place the rosette layer on top. Arrange the 16 iced pieces in fan shaped formation between the rosettes (see photograph).

# Strawberry cheesecake with cream

## Ingredients

For the mixture:
*1 pkt of crumble mix*
*1 egg*
*100g/4oz/¼lb margarine*

For the filling:
*25g/1oz/2tbs gelatine powder*
*6x15ml/6tbs/8tbs cold water*
*500g/1lb/1lb strawberries*
*500g/1lb/1lb curd cheese (quark)*
*250ml/8fl oz/1 cup milk*
*150g/5oz/5oz castor sugar*
*(fine granulated)*
*grated rind and juice from*
*1 lemon*
*500ml/18fl oz/2¼ cups double*
*cream (heavy cream)*

## Method

Preheat oven to 180°C/350°F/Gas 4.

1   To make the mixture: Follow the instructions on the packet to make the crumble mix. Put ⅔ of the mix in a greased and lined spring-release tin (25cm/10"). Press down gently. Cook for 15 minutes.

2   Directly after baking loosen the cake from the tin with a knife, and put on to a wire rack to cool. Line the sides of the cake tin with a strip of greaseproof paper. Replace the baked layer.

3   Sprinkle the rest of the crumble mix on to a greased baking sheet and cook until golden for about 10 minutes.

4   To make the filling: Stir the gelatine powder into a pan with cold water and leave to soak for 10 minutes.

5   Wash and hull the strawberries and leave to drain. Cut in halves or quarters.

6   Beat the cheese, milk, sugar, lemon rind and juice together until well mixed.

7   Heat the soaked gelatine stirring all the while until completely dissolved. Leave to cool a little then stir into the mixture.

8   Whip the cream until stiff. Fold in the cheese mixture. Spread half evenly over the cake then distribute the strawberries over the top. Leave an empty border around the edge of the cake. Cover the strawberries with the rest of the mixture. Spread smoothly and then sprinkle the crumble mix on top.

9   Put the cake in a cool place. After about 2 hours remove the side of the tin and greaseproof paper.

**Fruit flans
and tarts**

# Macaroon flan with strawberries

(illustrated pages 28-29)

## Ingredients

For the pastry:
*100g/4oz/¼lb plain flour
(all purpose)
1x2.5ml/½tsp/½tsp baking
powder
50g/2oz/4tbs castor sugar
(fine granulated)
1x5ml/1tsp/1tsp vanilla essence
(extract)
2 egg yolks
75g/3oz/6tbs cold butter*

For the filling and topping:
*2 egg whites
150g/5oz/5oz castor sugar
(fine granulated)
175g/6oz/6oz ground almonds
750g/1½lb/1½lb strawberries
red wine
1 pkt red Quick Jel fruit flan
glaze
250ml/8fl oz/1 cup fruit juice*

Decoration:
*whipped cream*

## Method

Preheat oven to 200°C/400°F/Gas 6.

1   Sift the flour and baking powder on to a pastry board and
    make a hollow in the middle. Put the sugar, vanilla and yolks
    into the centre. Work some of the flour into the mixture until it
    is a thick paste. Cut the butter into small pieces, add to the

mixture, dust with flour and working from the centre, quickly knead all the ingredients into a smooth dough. If the dough is sticky, place it in a refrigerator to become firm.

2  Roll out to fit a spring-release cake tin base (25cm/10"). Prick dough several times with a fork. Bake until golden brown, for about 15 minutes.

3  To make the filling and topping: Preheat oven to 150°C/300°F/Gas 3. Beat whites until they are foamy. Gradually beat in 100g/4oz/¼lb sugar. Carefully fold in almonds.

4  Fill a bag with this mixture and pipe around the edge of the baked and cooled base. Make an even wall of about 2.5cm/4" high. Place in preheated oven and bake for about 30-40 minutes.

5  Wash, hull and drain the strawberries well. Mix with rest of the sugar. Put into a strainer over a basin and leave for 30 minutes.

6  Arrange the fruit over the flan.

7  Combine the strawberry juice with red wine to make up 250ml/8fl oz/1 cup.

8  Take the fruit flan glaze and mix with sugar and strawberry wine liquid according to the instructions on the packet.

9  Brush or pour the glaze over the strawberries and decorate with whipped cream.

# Fruit flan

## Ingredients

For the flan:
75g/3oz/6tbs butter or firm
margarine
75g/3oz/6tbs castor sugar
(fine granulated)
1x5ml/1tsp/1tsp vanilla essence
(extract)
2 eggs, lightly beaten
salt
100g/4oz/¼lb plain flour
(all purpose)
1x5ml/1tsp/1tsp baking powder
2x15ml/2tbs/3tbs apricot jam
(jelly)

For the filling:
500g/1lb/1lb fresh fruit
(e.g. kiwifruit, strawberries, bil-
berries, grapes).
castor sugar (fine granulated)

For the glaze:
1 pkt Quick Jel flan glaze
castor sugar (fine granulated)
250ml/8fl oz/1 cup water or
fruit juice

## Method

Preheat oven to 180°C/350°F/Gas 4.

1   To make the flan: Cream together the butter or margine, sugar and vanilla.

2   Sift together the salt, flour and baking powder and gradually mix in the eggs. Beat into the butter-sugar mixture a little at a time.

3   Grease a flan tin (25cm/10") and pour in the mixture. Bake for 20-30 minutes until golden.

4   When the flan is cool, brush with apricot jam to prevent the base of the flan becoming soggy when the fruit is put in.

5   Rinse the fruit if necessary. Drain well, slice if large, sprinkle with sugar and leave to stand for a while. Arrange in the flan case.

6   To make the glaze: Mix the glaze with sugar and water or fruit juice, according to the instructions on the packet.

7   Pour or brush the glaze over the fruit.

# Fruit tartlets

(12 - 14 tartlets diam. about 10cm/4" illustrated page 33)

**Ingredients**

For the pastry:
*175g/6oz/6oz plain flour
(all purpose)
1x5ml/1tsp/1tsp baking powder
75g/3oz/3oz castor sugar
(fine granulated)
1x5ml/1tsp/1tsp vanilla essence
(extract)
salt
4 drops lemon essence (extract)
2x15ml/2tbs/3tbs water
100g/4oz/¼lb butter or
firm margarine
3x15ml/3tbs/4tbs apricot jam
(jelly)*

For the filling:
*preserved or bottled fruit,
e.g pineapple, apricots,
peaches, gooseberries,
tangerines, Morello cherries
1 pkt Quick Jel flan glaze
castor sugar (fine granulated)
250ml/8fl oz/1 cup water or
fruit juice
250ml/8fl oz/1 cup double
cream (heavy cream)
1x5ml/1tsp/1tsp vanilla essence
(extract)*

**Method**
Preheat oven to 180°C/350°F/Gas 4.
1   To make the pastry: Sift the flour and baking powder on to a pastry board and make a hollow in the middle. Add the sugar, vanilla, salt, lemon essence, and water. Work the ingredients into part of the flour until it is a thick paste.
2   Cut the butter into small pieces and add to the mixture.
    Dust with flour and working from the centre, quickly knead all the ingredients into a smooth dough. Chill until firm.
3   Roll the dough to a thickness of about 3mm/⅛". Cut out rounds with a pastry cutter and prick with a fork. Bake for 10-15 minutes or until golden.
4   When the tartlets are cooked, brush them with apricot jam to prevent them from becoming soggy when lined with fruit.
5   To make the filling: Drain the fruit and arrange it on the tartlets (leave a 1cm/½" space around the edges).
6   Make up the flan glaze adding sugar and fruit juice or water according to the directions on the packet. Spread or brush the glaze over the fruit.

7   Whip the cream and vanilla until stiff and pipe rosettes around the tartlets.


# Apricot cheese flan

### Ingredients

*1 pkt shortcrust pastry mix*

For the filling and glaze:
*225g/8oz/¹/₂lb curd cheese*
*50g/2oz/4tbs castor sugar (fine granulated)*
*1x5ml/1tsp/1tsp vanilla essence (extract)*
*3 drops lemon essence (extract)*

*2 eggs*
*50g/2oz/4tbs ground almonds*
*15g/¹/₂oz/1tbs cornflour (cornstarch)*
*500g/1lb/1lb bottled apricots or lightly cooked apricots*
*1x15ml/1tbs/2tbs apricot jam (jelly)*
*1x15ml/1tbs/2tbs water*

### Method

Preheat oven to 180°C/350°F/Gas 4.

1   To make the flan pastry: make the flan dough according to the instructions on the packet. Roll out ²/₃ of it on to a greased spring-release cake tin base (diameter about 23cm/9''). Shape the remaining dough into a roll. Form into a ring around the edge of the flan base and press down to make an upright edge of about 2cm/³/₄''.

2   For the filling: Stir together cheese, sugar, vanilla, lemon essence, eggs, ground almonds and cornflour. Spread over the flan base.

3   Drain the apricots and arrange in a circle on top of the mixture. Bake in a preheated oven for about 45-50 minutes until firm and golden.

4   Boil up apricot jam with the water. Brush the flan with it immediately.

# Grape flan with meringue topping

**Ingredients**

For the flan:
*1 pkt sponge mix*

For the filling:
*120ml/4fl oz/¹/₂ cup confectioners
custard (pastry cream)
750g/1¹/₂lbs/1¹/₂lbs white grapes
40g/1¹/₂tbs/3tbs castor sugar
(fine granulated)
1x5ml/1tsp/1tsp vanilla essence
(extract)
white wine
1 pkt Quick Jel flan glaze*

For the meringue topping:
*2 egg whites
100g/4oz/¹/₄lb castor sugar
(fine granulated)*

**Method**

Preheat oven to 180°C/350°F/Gas 4.
1   To make the flan: Make up the sponge according to
    instructions on packet. Line a greased sandwich tin (23cm/9")
    with foil. Pour in the mixture. Bake for 25-30 minutes.
2   To make the filling: Spread the custard in the flan.
3   Wash, halve and remove pips from the grapes. Mix them with
    sugar and vanilla. Put them into a strainer over a bowl to catch
    the juice.
4   Add white wine to the grape juice to make up 250ml/8fl oz/
    1 cup liquid.
5   Arrange the grapes on the flan. Make the glaze according to
    the instructions on the packet. Pour over the grapes and leave
    to cool.

6 To make the meringue topping: Beat the egg whites until stiff. Whisk in sugar gradually. Pipe the mixture on to the grapes.
7 Put on a grid under a preheated grill or place for 10 minutes on the top shelf of a hot oven to colour the meringue.

# Gooseberry meringue tartlets

## Ingredients

For the filling:
*500g/1lb/1lb gooseberries*
*150g/5oz/5oz castor sugar*
*(fine granulated)*
*600ml/1pt/2½ cups water*

For the meringue:
*2 egg whites*
*100g/4oz/¼lb castor sugar*
*(fine granulated)*

For the glaze:
*1 pkt Quick Jel flan glaze*
*250ml/8fl oz/1 cup gooseberry*
*juice (extended with water if necessary)*

## Method

Preheat oven to 100°C/200°F/Gas 1.

1  To make the filling: Top and tail the gooseberries. Wash and drain, and place in water with sugar. Simmer the gooseberries while stirring carefully (they must not break).

2  To make the meringue: Beat the egg whites until stiff. Gradually whisk in the sugar until very stiff.

3  Fill a piping bag fitted with rose nozzle with the mixture and pipe spiral-shaped tartlets (7.5 cm/3") on to a baking sheet covered with foil. Pipe a rosette on to each tartlet. The rosette of meringue is intended to cap the fruit. Bake 30 minutes - turn off heat and leave in oven until cool.

4  To make the glaze: Make the flan glaze according to the instructions on the packet, using 250ml/8fl oz/1 cup of gooseberry juice (extended with water if necessary). Spread the glaze over the gooseberries in the tartlets. Serve with whipped cream.

# Apricot almond flan

## Ingredients

For the flan pastry:
*100g/4oz/¼lb cold butter or*
*firm margarine*
*225g/8oz/½lb plain flour*
*(all purpose)*
*75g/3oz/6tbs castor sugar*
*(fine granulated)*
*1x5ml/1tsp/1tsp vanilla essence*
*(extract)*
*salt*
*1 egg*

For the filling and topping:
*100g/4oz/¼lb ground almonds*
*100g/4oz/¼lb castor sugar*
*(fine granulated)*
*1 egg*
*120ml/4fl oz/½ cup double*
*cream (heavy cream)*
*500g/1lb/1lb lightly cooked or*
*bottled apricots*
*blanched almonds, halved*

For the apricot glaze:
*1x15ml/1tbs/2tbs apricot jam*
*(jelly)*
*1x15ml/1tbs/2tbs water*

## Method

Preheat oven to 180°C/350°F/Gas 4.

1  To make the pastry: Mix the flour and baking powder. Sift onto a pastry board and make a hollow in the middle of the flour.
2  Put the sugar, vanilla, salt and egg into the centre and work in part of the flour until it becomes a thick paste. Cut the butter into pieces, add to the paste, dust with flour and working from the centre, knead all the ingredients into a smooth dough. Chill until firm.
3  Roll out the dough to fit a spring-release cake tin base, (23cm/9") and pinch up the edge to make an upright rim of about 1cm/½" height.
4  To make the filling and topping: Stir together the almonds, sugar, egg and cream until frothy. Pour the mixture over the flan base.
5  Drain the apricots and arrange with the hollow side upwards

over the flan. Place one almond half in each hollow.
Bake for about 45 minutes.

6  For the apricot glaze: Sieve the jam, stir in water and bring to the boil - brush over the flan.
As soon as the flan is out of the oven, spread it with the apricot glaze.

# Pear flan with cassis cream

## Ingredients

For the flan pastry:
*225g/8oz/½lb plain flour*
*(all purpose)*
*75g/3oz/6tbs castor sugar*
*(fine granulated)*
*1x5ml/1tsp/1tsp vanilla essence*
*(extract)*
*150g/5oz/5oz cold butter or*
*firm margarine*

For the filling and topping:
*500g/1lb/1lb/cooked or bottled pears*
*2x15ml/2tbs/3tbs cassis*
*350ml/12fl oz/1½cups double*
*cream (heavy cream) chilled*
*25g/1oz/2tbs castor sugar*
*(fine granulated)*
*grated chocolate*

## Method

Preheat oven to 180°C/350°F/Gas 4.

1   To make flan pastry: Sieve the flour onto a pastry board, make a hollow in the middle of the flour. Add sugar and vanilla.

2   Cut the butter or margarine in pieces and add dust with the flour. Working from the centre incorporate the flour and make a smooth dough. Wrap in clingfilm and chill.

3   Roll out a generous portion of the dough to fit a greased, spring-release cake tin base (23cm/9"). Shape the remaining dough into a long roll. Fit this as a ring around the edge of the flan and press down so that there is a circular ridge of almost 2.5cm/1" height. Prick base with fork.
    Directly after baking, loosen the cake from the cake tin base.

4   To make the filling and topping: Drain the pears, slice and arrange on the flan.

5   Beat the chilled cream for half a minute, add sugar and beat until stiff.
6   Fill a piping bag with half of the cream.
7   Fold the cassis into the remaining cream and spread the mixture smoothly over the pears.
8   Pipe rosettes of cream around the edge and garnish with chocolate.

# Redcurrant meringue flan

## Ingredients

For the flan:
*1 pkt flan mix*

For the glaze:
*1pkt Quick Jel fruit flan glaze*
*250ml/8fl oz/1 cup redcurrant juice*

For the filling:
*500g/1lb/1lb redcurrants*
*100g/4oz/¼lb castor sugar*
*2x15ml/2tbs/3tbs redcurrant jelly*

For the meringue:
*1 egg white*
*50g/2oz/4tbs castor sugar (fine granulated)*

## Method

Preheat oven to 180°C/350°F/Gas 4.

1   To make the flan: Make the sponge according to the instructions on the packet. Grease a flan tin (23cm/9") and pour in the mixture. Bake for approx 25 minutes.

2   After baking leave the flan to cool and cover the base with heated redcurrant jelly.

3   To make the filling: Mix the redcurrants with sugar. Put them into a strainer over a bowl to catch the juice. Leave until they are well drained, then arrange them in the flan.

4   To make the glaze: Make the glaze according to the instructions on the Quick Jel packet with the redcurrant juice. Pour the glaze over the redcurrants and leave to cool.

5   To make the meringue: Beat the egg white until stiff. Whisk in the sugar a little at a time. Pipe the meringue mixture over the top of the flan.

6   Place the flan under a preheated grill for about 3 minutes, or on the top shelf of a hot oven for 10 minutes, to colour the meringue.

# Apple sponge flan

## Ingredients

For the flan pastry:
*150g/5oz/5oz plain flour
(all purpose)
40g/1½oz/3tbs castor sugar
(fine granulated)
1x5ml/1tsp/1tsp vanilla essence
(extract)
100g/4oz/¼lb cold butter or
firm margarine*

For the filling and topping:
*500g/1lb/1lb Cox's Orange Pippin apples
250ml/8fl oz/1 cup white wine
120ml/4fl oz/½ cup water
50g/2oz/4tbs castor sugar
(fine granulated)
1x5ml/1tsp/1tsp vanilla essence
(extract)
1 stick of cinnamon
3x15ml/3tbs/4tbs redcurrant
jelly*

For the sponge:
*2 egg yolks
3x15ml/3tbs/4tbs lukewarm
water
100g/4oz/¼lb castor sugar
(fine granulated)
1x5ml/1tsp/1tsp vanilla essence
(extract)
2 egg whites
75g/3oz/6tbs plain flour
(all purpose)
50g/2oz/4tbs cornflour
(cornstarch)
1x5ml/1tsp/1tsp baking powder*

For the glaze:
*1 pkt Quick Jel clear glaze
25g/1oz/2tbs castor sugar
(fine granulated)*

Decoration:
*whipped cream (optional)*

## Method

Preheat oven to 180°C/350°F/Gas 4.
1  To make the pastry: Sieve the flour onto a pastry board, make a hollow in the middle. Add sugar and vanilla. Cut the butter or margarine into pieces, dust with flour and working from the centre, quickly knead all the ingredients into a smooth dough.

2  Chill until firm. Roll out the dough to fit a greased, spring-release cake tin base (23cm/9''). Prick the base and bake for 20 minutes.

3  When cooked remove from tin, leave to cool.

4   To make the sponge: Whisk yolks with water until frothy.
    Gradually add ⅔ of the sugar and vanilla, whisk until creamy.
    Beat egg whites until stiff then whisk in rest of sugar.
    Fold whites into the mixture. Pour into a greased, spring-
    release cake tin base (23cm/9") lined with greaseproof paper.
    Bake for 20-30 minutes.

5   To make the filling and topping: Peel, quarter and core the
    apples, slice thickly. Simmer with white wine, water, sugar,
    vanilla and stick of cinnamon but do not allow to get pulpy.

6   Spread the pastry base with redcurrant jelly. Put the sponge
    layer on top and arrange the apples on the sponge in a circle.

7   For the glaze: Make up the glaze according to the instructions
    on packet, with the sugar and fruit juice. Pour the glaze evenly
    over the apples.
    If required, decorate the apple sponge flan with whipped
    cream.

# Apple or cherry pie

## Ingredients

For the pastry:
*275g/10oz/10oz plain flour
(all purpose)
2x5ml/2tsp/2tsp baking powder
100g/4oz/¼lb castor sugar
(fine granulated)
1x5ml/1tsp/1tsp vanilla essence
(extract)
salt
½ egg yolk
1 egg white
1x15ml/1tbs/2tbs milk
150g/5oz/5oz cold butter or
firm margarine*

For the glaze:
*½ egg yolk
1x15ml/1tbs/2tbs milk*

For the apple filling:
*50g/2oz/4tbs raisins
2x5ml/2tbs/3tbs baking powder
1kg/2lb/2lb Bramley apples
1x15ml/1tbs/2tbs water
100g/4oz/¼lb castor sugar
(fine granulated)
1x2.5ml/1tsp/1tsp ground
cinnamon
few drops rum or lemon
essence (extract)*

For the cherry filling:
*1kg/2lb/2lb Morello cherries
100g/4oz/¼lb castor sugar
(fine granulated)
25g/1oz/2tbs cornflour
(cornstarch)
1x15ml/1tbs/2tbs sugar (for
flavouring)*

## Method

Preheat oven to 180°C/350°F/Gas 4.
1   To make the pastry: Mix together the flour and baking powder.
    Sieve on to a pastry board and make a hollow in the middle.
    Add sugar, vanilla, salt, ½ egg yolk, egg white and milk.

2   Work into part of the flour until it is a thick paste. Cut the
    butter into pieces and add to the mixture. Dust with flour and
    working from the centre outwards, quickly knead all the
    ingredients into a smooth dough. Wrap in clingfilm and chill.

3   Take a little less than half of the dough and roll it out to fit a
    greased, spring-release cake tin base (23cm/9").
    Prick base with a fork and bake for 25-30 minutes.

4   To make the apple filling: Peel, core and quarter the apples, and slice. Simmer the apple slices with water, sugar, cinnamon and raisins. Leave to cool a little and flavour with a few drops of rum or lemon essence.

5   To make the cherry filling: Rinse and stone the cherries. Mix with sugar and boil briefly, then drain and leave the cherries and juice to cool.

6   Measure 250ml/8fl oz/1 cup juice (if necessary extend with water). Blend cornflour with the juice, bring to the boil whilst stirring constantly. Cook briefly then stir in the cherries. Leave to cool and flavour with sugar.

7   Roll out the rest of the dough and cut it to fit a spring-release cake tin base. Use the remaining dough to roll out a long roll of finger thickness. Place this as a ring around the edge of the baked pie base, to form a ridge about 2.5cm/1" high. Spread the chosen filling over the base and lay the rolled out pastry on top.

8   Stir the egg yolk lightly with milk. Brush the pastry with this mixture and prick lightly several times with a fork.
Bake for 30 minutes until golden.

**Cakes for
special occasions**

# Butter cream cake

(illustrated pages 50/51)

**Ingredients**

For the mixture:
*3 egg yolks*
*3x15ml/3tbs/4tbs warm water*
*150g/4oz/1/4lb castor sugar*
*1x5ml/1tsp/1tsp vanilla essence (extract)*
*3 egg whites*
*100g/4oz/1/4lb plain flour*
*(all purpose)*
*100g/4oz/1/4lb cornflour*
*(cornstarch)*

For the filling and topping:
*750ml/1 1/4pts/3cups confectioners*
*custard (pastry cream)*
*225g/8oz/1/2lb butter or margarine*
*100g/4oz/1/4lb plain dark chocolate*
*2x15ml/2tbs/3tbs apricot jam (jelly)*
*pistachio nuts, halved*

**Method**

Preheat oven to 180°C/350°F/Gas 4.

1  To make the mixture: Whisk the egg yolks with warm water until frothy. Gradually add ⅔ of sugar and vanilla. Beat until the mixture is creamy. Whisk egg whites until stiff. Add the remaining sugar a little at a time. Fold the egg white into the yolk mixture. Sift together the flour, cornflour and baking powder and fold in.

2  Use a greased, spring-release cake tin base covered with greaseproof paper (23cm/9''). Pour in the mixture and bake for 30 minutes until golden. Leave to cool after baking.

3  To make the filling and topping: Cream the butter until soft and light, beat in the confectioners custard a little at a time.

(Take care that neither the butter nor the custard are too cold as the mixture will curdle.)

4   Cut the cake through twice, to make 3 layers.

5   Put the chocolate in a bowl over a pan of hot water. Stir until the chocolate melts into a smooth mixture. Spread the bottom layer with chocolate then with a quarter of the vanilla cream. Put on the second layer of cake. Spread with apricot jam then with a portion of the remaining vanilla cream. Cover with the third layer of cake. Spread the edge and top of the cake thinly and evenly with some of the remaining vanilla cream. Fit a piping bag with a star nozzle, fill with remaining cream and decorate cake. Garnish with halved pistachio nuts.

# Furrow cake
(illustrated page 55)

## Ingredients

For the mixture:
*4 egg yolks*
*4x15ml/4tbs/5tbs warm water*
*100g/4oz/¼lb sugar*
*1x5ml/1tsp/1tsp vanilla essence*
*(extract)*
*4 egg whites*
*50g/2oz/4tbs plain flour*
*(all purpose)*
*50g/2oz/4tbs cornflour*
*(cornstarch)*
*25g/1oz/2tbs cocoa*
*1x2.5ml/½tsp/½tsp baking*
*powder*

For the nougat:
*1 nut of butter*
*25g/1oz/2tbs castor sugar*
*(fine granulated)*
*50g/2oz/4tbs blanched*
*almonds, chopped*
*oil*

For the filling and topping:
*500ml/18fl oz/2¼ cups milk*
*40g/1½oz/3tbs cornflour*
*(cornstarch)*
*100g/4oz/¼lb castor sugar*
*(fine granulated)*
*225g/8oz/½lb butter*
*cocoa*
*6x15ml/6tbs/8tbs rum*
*175g/6oz/6oz redcurrant jelly*

53

**Method**

Preheat oven to 190°C/375°F/Gas 5.

1   To make the mixture: Whisk the yolks and water until frothy. Gradually add ⅔ of the sugar and vanilla. Whisk until the mixture is creamy. Beat whites until stiff, gradually add remaining sugar and fold into the yolks. Mix together the flour, cornflour, cocoa and baking powder.

2   Sift and fold into the mixture (do not stir). Spread the mixture about 1cm/½" thick on a baking sheet covered with greaseproof paper. Lay a folded strip of aluminium foil along the front of the mixture. Bake for 10-15 minutes until well risen and firm.

3   Turn out the cake immediately on to a layer of paper sprinkled with castor sugar. Brush the greaseproof paper with cold water and pull carefully but swiftly from the bottom of the cake.

4   To make the nougat: Melt the butter and sugar. Heat gently whilst stirring until the sugar is light brown. Stir in the almonds, heat until the nougat is golden. Pour onto a flat plate greased with oil, leave until set and cold then crush the nougat.

5   To make the filling and topping: Take 5x15ml/5tbs/6tbs of milk. Blend the rest of the milk with cornflour and sugar. Bring the rest of the milk to the boil. Take off the heat and slowly pour in the blended cornflour. Boil up once then leave to cool, stirring occasionally.

6   Cream the butter until it is fluffy and whisk in the custard. Stir 3x15ml/3tbs/4tbs of this cream together with cocoa and fill a piping bag.

7   Sprinkle the cake layer with rum.

8   Stir the redcurrant jelly until it is smooth. Spread the cake layer first with the jelly and then with ⅔ of the custard. Cut the cake layer lengthways in 6 strips about 5cm/2" wide. Roll up the first strip of cake, then set it upright in circular form. Cut the other strips in half and add to the circles so that a circular cake is formed.

9   Spread the sides and top of the cake with the remaining custard. Sprinkle the sides with nougat. Trace circular furrows with a fork around the top of the cake. Pipe a decorative edge around the cake with the cream in the piping bag.

# Frankfurter ring

## Ingredients

For the mixture:
*100g/4oz/¼lb butter or
margarine
150g/5oz/5oz sugar
3 eggs
salt
4 drops lemon essence (extract)
or rum essence (extract)
150g/5oz/5oz plain flour
(all purpose)
50g/2oz/4tbs cornflour
(cornstarch)
1x5ml/1tsp/1tsp baking powder*

For the nougat:
*knob of butter
50g/2oz/4tbs castor sugar
(fine granulated)
100g/4oz/¼lb chopped
almonds, blanched*

Decoration:
*glacé cherries*

For the filling and topping:
*600ml/1pt/2 ½ cups
confectioners custard
(pastry cream)
175g/6oz/6oz butter or
margarine*

## Method

Preheat oven to 180°C/350°F/Gas 4.
1   To make the mixture: Cream the butter until light and fluffy.
    Gradually add sugar, eggs, salt and lemon or rum essence.
    Sift together flour, cornflour and baking powder. Sift and fold
    into the butter mixture. Put into a greased ring-tin.
    Bake for 35-45 minutes.
2   To make the filling and topping: Cream the butter until fluffy.
    Beat in the custard spoonful by spoonful (take care that neither
    are too cold as curdling will occur).
3   To make the nougat: Melt butter and sugar. Heat gently whilst
    stirring, until the sugar is light brown. Stir in the almonds.
    Heat whilst stirring until the nougat is golden brown. Pour
    onto a flat plate greased with oil.

56

4   When cold and set, crush the nougat.
5   Cut the cake through twice. Spread the layers of cake with the butter cream filling. Spread the outside of the cake with butter cream (putting a little aside). Sprinkle with nougat. Decorate with the remaining butter cream and with glacé cherries if desired.

# Crème de la crème cake

## Ingredients

For the mixture:
225g/8oz/½lb butter or margarine
225g/8oz/½lb castor sugar (fine granulated)
1x5ml/1tsp/1tsp vanilla essence (extract)
4 eggs
salt
175g/6oz/6oz plain flour (all purpose)
50g/2oz/4tbs cornflour (cornstarch)
1x5ml/1tsp/1tsp baking powder

For the butter cream filling:
500ml/18fl oz/2 ¼ cups chocolate flavoured confectioners custard (pastry cream), warm
175g/6oz/6oz butter or margarine

For the icing (frosting):
100g/4oz/¼lb chocolate
knob of butter

Decoration:
chocolate squares

## Method

Preheat oven to 180°C/350°F/Gas 4.

1   To make the mixture: Beat the butter or margarine until fluffy. Gradually add sugar, vanilla, eggs and salt. Sift together flour, cornflour and baking powder. Fold into the butter mixture.

2   Use mixture to make 8 cake layers. Spread 2x15ml/2tbs/3tbs of the mixture on to a greased spring-release cake tin base (23cm/9") to make each cake layer. Take care that the mixture is not too thin around the edges. Bake until the cake is golden, about 8-10 minutes.

3   To make the cream butter filling: Beat the butter until fluffy. Stir in the custard. Spread each layer of cake with butter cream (set aside 3x15ml/3tbs/4tbs for decoration). Sandwich the layers together to make a cake.

4   To make the icing (frosting): Put chocolate and butter in a bowl over a pan of hot water. Stir it until it has melted to a smooth mixture.

5   Cover the cake with the chocolate icing and decorate with the remaining butter cream and chocolate squares.

# Panama cake

## Ingredients

For the mixture:
*150g/5oz/5oz plain dark chocolate*
*7 eggs*
*150g/5oz/5oz castor sugar*
*(fine granulated)*
*1x5ml/1tsp/1tsp vanilla essence*
*(extract)*
*25g/1oz/2tbs plain flour*
*(all purpose)*
*1x5ml/1tsp/1tsp baking powder*
*150g/5oz/5oz ground hazelnuts*

For the filling and icing
(frosting):
*150g/5oz/5oz butter*
*50g/2oz/4tbs icing sugar*
*(confectioners)*
*2 eggs*
*100g/4oz/¼lb plain dark chocolate*

Decoration:
*25g/1oz/2tbs flaked almonds, toasted*
*chocolate (optional)*

## Method

Preheat oven to 160°C/325°F/Gas 3.
1   To make the mixture: Break the chocolate into pieces and put
    into a bowl over a pan of hot water. Stir until smooth.
    Whisk the eggs. Mix sugar and vanilla together. Sprinkle it into
    the chocolate mixture and whisk for 2 more minutes.
    Mix together and sift the flour and baking powder, add
    hazelnuts and fold into the chocolate mixture. Carry on with
    the electric mixer at the slowest speed, for a short while. Put
    the mixture into a greased spring-release cake tin (about

23cm/9"). Bake until risen and firm, about 50 minutes. Leave cake to cool after baking.

2 To make the filling and icing (frosting): Cream the butter until fluffy. Sieve the icing sugar, add gradually with eggs to the butter. Break chocolate in pieces. Put into a bowl over a pan of hot water and stir until it is smooth.
Gradually fold the butter cream into the chocolate.

3 Cut the cake through once. Spread the bottom layer with half the butter cream chocolate. Put on the other layer.
Spread the top and sides with the remaining chocolate butter cream. Make furrows with a fork in the top of the cake.

4 Sprinkle the sides of the cake with the toasted almonds and if desired, decorate the cake with chocolates.

# Chocolate almond cake

## Ingredients

For the mixture:
*1 pkt chocolate sponge cake mix*

For the filling:
*500ml/18fl oz/2¼ cups chocolate flavoured
confectioners custard (pastry cream), warm
175g/6oz/6oz butter or margarine*

For the glaze and decoration:
*1x15ml/1tbs/2tbs apricot jam (jelly)
50g/2oz/2oz toasted almonds, flaked*

## Method

Preheat oven to 180°C/350°F/Gas 4.

1  Make the chocolate sponge according to the instructions on the
   packet. Pour into a greased spring-release tin (23cm/9").
   Bake as instructed. After baking remove the sides of the tin
   and leave the cake to cool on a wire tray.

2  To make the filling: Cut the butter into pieces. Beat into the
   chocolate mixture.

3  Cut the cake through twice. Spread the layers of cake with
   chocolate cream and sandwich them together. Spread the sides
   and top with the apricot jam and sprinkle with almonds.

# Praline cake

## Ingredients

For the mixture:
175g/6oz/6oz butter
175g/6oz/6oz castor sugar
(fine granulated)
1x5ml/1tsp/1tsp vanilla essence
(extract)
4 eggs
1x5ml/1tsp/1tsp rum essence
(extract)
175g/6oz/6oz plain flour
(all purpose)
15g/½oz/1 tbs cocoa
2x5ml/2tsp/2tsp baking powder

For the filling and topping:
450ml/¾pt/2 cups
confectioners custard
(pastry cream)
2x15ml/2tbs/3tbs brandy
100g/4oz/¼lb chocolate

Decoration:
50g/2oz/4tbs grated chocolate
and 16 chocolates

## Method

Preheat oven to 180°C/350°F/Gas 4.
1  To make the mixture: Cream the butter until fluffy. Stir in
   sugar, vanilla, eggs and rum essence. Mix together the flour,
   cocoa and baking powder. Sift and fold into the butter mixture.
   Pour into a greased spring-release cake tin (23cm/9").
   Bake for about 40 minutes. Leave cake to cool.
2  To make the filling and topping: Stir the brandy into the
   custard. Break the chocolate into pieces, warm it in a bowl over
   a pan of hot water until it is soft. Stir the custard into the
   chocolate.
3  Cut the cake through once. Spread the bottom layer with half
   the chocolate cream. Put the other layer of cake on top. Press
   down gently. Spread the outside of the cake with chocolate
   cream, retaining some cream for decoration. Sprinkle the
   outsides of the cake with grated chocolate.
4  Decorate the cake with 16 chocolates and the rest of the
   chocolate cream.

# Heart cake

## Ingredients

For the mixture:
*75g/3oz/6tbs butter*
*100g/4oz/¼lb castor sugar*
*(fine granulated)*
*1x5ml/1tsp/1tsp vanilla essence*
*(extract)*
*2 eggs*
*salt*
*100g/4oz/¼lb plain flour*
*(all purpose)*
*25g/1oz/2tbs cornflour*
*(cornstarch)*
*1x5ml/1tsp/1tsp baking powder*

For the icing (frosting):
*100g/4oz/ ¼lb chocolate*
*knob of butter*

For the filling:
*1x15ml/1tbs/2tbs jam (jelly)*
*50g/2oz/2oz almond paste*
*(marzipan)*
*25g/1oz/2tbs sifted icing sugar*
*(confectioners)*
*350ml/12floz/1½ cups*
*confectioners custard*
*(pastry cream)*
*150g/5oz/5oz butter*

Decoration:
*chocolate flakes and*
*coloured sugar flowers*

## Method

Preheat oven to 180°C/350°F/Gas 4.

1   To make the mixture: Cream the butter until fluffy, gradually beat in sugar, vanilla, eggs and salt. Mix together the flour, cornflour and baking powder. Sift and fold into the butter mixture. Pour into a greased and lined heart-shaped cake tin. Bake for about 30 minutes until well risen and golden. Turn out the cake, cool and cut through twice.

2   To make the icing: Put the chocolate and butter into a bowl over a pan of hot water and stir until it is smooth. Spread over the top layer of cake.

3   To make the filling: Knead the almond paste and icing sugar together and roll it out flat. Cut a heart shape to fit.

4   Spread the middle layer of cake with jam. Place almond paste on top and press down gently.

5   Cream the butter until fluffy. Gradually beat in the confectioners custard. Fill a piping bag fitted with a plain

nozzle with 2x15ml/2tbs/3tbs of the mixture. Cover the bottom layer of cake with ⅓ of the cream. Put middle layer on top and pipe cream on this. Cover the sides of the cake with cream. Put iced layer on top.

6  Sprinkle sides of cake with chocolate flakes. Decorate top of cake with cream from the piping bag. Decorate with chocolate flakes and coloured sugar flowers.

# Cherry snow cake

**Ingredients**

For the biscuit dough:
*4 egg yolks*
*3x15ml/3tbs/4tbs warm water*
*100g/4oz/¼lb castor sugar*
*(fine granulated)*
*1x5ml/1tsp/1tsp baking powder*
*1x5ml/1tsp/1tsp vanilla essence*
*(extract)*
*1 egg white*
*75g/3oz/6tbs plain flour*
*(all purpose)*
*50g/2oz/4tbs cornflour*
*(cornstarch)*

For soaking the biscuit layer:
*6x15ml/6tbs/8tbs water*
*50g/2oz/4tbs castor sugar*
*(fine granulated)*
*6x15ml/6tbs/8tbs Kirsch*

For the cake:
*3 egg whites*
*150g/5oz/5oz castor sugar*
*(fine granulated)*
*1x5ml/1tsp/1tsp vanilla essence (extract)*
*100g/4oz/¼lb ground almonds*

For the filling:
*450ml/³/₄pt/2 cups raspberry*
*flavoured confectioners custard*
*(pastry cream)*
*150g/5oz/5oz butter or*
*margarine*

Garnish:
*50g/2oz/4tbs flaked almonds*
*25g/1oz/2tbs icing sugar*
*(confectioners)*


**Method**

Preheat oven to 180°C/350°F/Gas 4.

1   To make the biscuit mixture: Stir the yolks and water until
    frothy, gradually add ⅔ of the sugar and vanilla. Beat until the
    mixture is creamy. Beat egg whites until stiff, gradually adding
    the remaining sugar and fold into the yolk mixture.

2   Sift together the flour, cornflour and baking powder and fold
    into the mixture. Pour on to a greased, spring-release cake base
    (23cm/9") covered by greased greaseproof paper. Bake for
    25-30 minutes. Leave the biscuit layer until cool.

3   To make the cake layer:
    Preheat oven to 100°C/200°F/Gas 1.
    Beat egg whites until stiff. Gradually whisk in sugar and
    vanilla. Carefully fold in the ground almonds. Divide the
    mixture in half. Put each half in a well greased, spring-release
    cake tin, lined with greaseproof paper (23cm/9").
    Spread the mixture smoothly and bake for 1 hour - turn heat
    off and leave in oven for 30 minutes.

4   When the cake layers are baked, turn them out. Brush the
    greaseproof paper with water and peel it off.

5   To make the filling: Cream the butter until fluffy. Whisk in the
    custard mixture.

6   For soaking the biscuit layer: Bring sugar and water to the boil,
    then allow to cool. Add Kirsch.

7   Spread one of the cake layers with ¼ of the custard. Lay the
    biscuit layer on top. Sprinkle the Kirsch mixture over the biscuit

layer. Spread with a little less than half of the cream. Cover with the second layer and press down well.
Spread the sides and top with the rest of the cream.

8    Toast the almonds on a baking sheet in the oven, until they are golden. Leave to cool and then sprinkle on the sides of the cake.

9    Dip a knife into hot water and use to trace a lattice pattern on top of the cake. Sift icing sugar evenly over the cake.
The cake is easy to cut if it is filled the day before it is to be eaten.

# A few important baking tips

A very important rule in baking is firstly read every recipe right through to the end.

Another tip - in preparation for baking a cake, set out all the necessary ingredients. This has the advantage that eggs, flour, sugar, baking powder and milk will all reach room temperature, which is beneficial to the baking result.

When is a cake ready? Before taking a cake out of the oven, it is a good idea to do the knitting needle test. Stick a knitting needle or skewer into the middle of the cake. If no damp crumbs stick to the needle when it is retrieved, then the cake is cooked and can be taken out of the oven.

Cake tins should be evenly greased at the beginning of a baking session. Then put the cake tins in the refrigerator. Thus the grease becomes hard and will not break when the tin is filled with cake mixture.

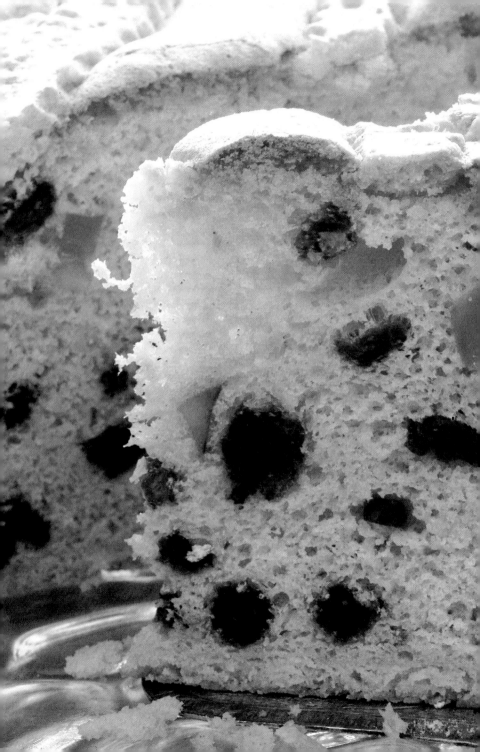

Classic cakes

# Cake of kings

(illustrated pages 72 - 73)

## Ingredients

For the biscuit mixture:
*225g/8oz/¹/₂lb plain flour
(all purpose)
1x5ml/1tsp/1tsp baking powder
75g/3oz/6tbs castor sugar
(fine granulated)
1x5ml/1tsp/1tsp vanilla essence
(extract)
2x15ml/2tbs/3tbs milk or water
100g/4oz/¹/₄lb cold butter or
firm margarine*

For the cake mixture:
*6 egg yolks
175g/6oz/6oz castor sugar
(fine granulated)
1x5ml/1tsp/1tsp vanilla
essence (extract)
1x5ml/1tsp/1tsp brandy or
rum essence (extract)
6 egg whites
225g/8oz/¹/₂lb plain flour
(all purpose)
1x5ml/1tsp/1tsp baking powder
100g/4oz/¹/₄lb chopped
almonds, blanched
175g/6oz/6oz raisins
100g/4oz/¹/₄lb candied peel,
chopped
100g/4oz/¹/₄lb butter or
margarine*

## Method

Preheat oven to 180°C/350°F/Gas 4.
1   To make biscuit mixture: Mix together the flour and baking
    powder. Sift on to a pastry board and make a hollow in the
    middle of the flour. Pour sugar, vanilla, milk or water into the
    hollow.
    Work into part of the flour until it becomes a thick paste.
    Cut butter or margarine into pieces. Add to the paste and dust
    with flour.
2   Working from the centre quickly knead all the ingredients into
    a smooth dough. Chill. Roll out ¹/₃ of the dough to fit a
    greased spring-release cake tin base (about 23cm/9"). Take a
    generous half of the rest of the dough and roll out a sheet to

fit the spring-release cake tin base. From this sheet of dough cut out 16 - 20 equally wide strips with a pastry wheel set aside. Make a finger thick roll and spread it as a ring around the dough on the cake tin base, press it down making an upright ridge of barely 2.5cm/1" high.

3　To make the cake mixture: Whisk 6 egg yolks lightly. Gradually add ⅔ of sugar and vanilla and whisk until the mixture is creamy. Stir in the brandy or rum essence.
Beat the whites until stiff. Gradually whisk in the rest of the sugar. Fold into the yolks. Sift together flour and baking powder and fold into the rest of the mixture. Add the almonds. Fold all the ingredients into the mixture (do not stir). Fold in gradually the melted and cooled butter or margarine.

4　Pour into the tin lined with the biscuit dough. Spread out the mixture smoothly and lay the strips of dough on top in a lattice pattern. Bake until well-risen and golden, 65 to 80 minutes.

# Some more important baking tips

If cake collapses after baking, this can have two causes.
Either you added more liquid to the cake mixture than the recipe stated, or you whisked too long with the mixer.
In both cases the mixture first rises well and then collapses after baking.

If cake sticks to the cake tin: Put the cake tin upside down on a wire tray. Put a damp tea cloth around the cake tin.
After a while the warmth of the tin plus the damp will have caused condensation to form in the tin so that the cake will leave the tin more easily.

# Fine chocolate cake

## Ingredients

For the mixture:
*150g/5oz/5oz butter*
*150/5oz/5oz castor sugar*
*(fine granulated)*
*1x5ml/1tsp/1tsp vanilla essence*
*(extract)*
*150g/5oz/5oz dark chocolate*
*6 eggs*
*150g/5oz/5oz plain flour*
*(all purpose)*
*25g/1oz/2tbs cocoa*
*1x5ml/1tsp/1tsp baking powder*

For the filling and icing
(frosting):
*6x15ml/6tbs/8tbs redcurrant jelly*
*100g/4oz/¼lb dark chocolate*
*5x15ml/5tbs/6tbs double*
*cream (heavy cream)*

## Method

Preheat oven to 180°C/350°F/Gas 4.
1   To make the mixture: Cream the butter until fluffy.
    Gradually beat in 75g/3oz/6tbs sugar, vanilla, melted chocolate,
    2 eggs and 4 egg yolks.

2   Mix together flour, cocoa and baking powder. Sift and fold
    into the butter mixture.

3   Beat 4 egg whites until stiff. Gradually whisk in remaining
    sugar. Carefully fold into the cake mixture. Pour into a spring-
    release cake tin (about 23cm/9'') lined with greaseproof paper.
    Spread smoothly. Bake until risen and firm, about 40 minutes.
    Turn out the cake, leave until cold.

Cut through once.

4  To make the filling and icing (frosting): Spread the bottom layer of cake with some redcurrant jelly. Cover with the top layer and spread the sides and top of the cake evenly with remaining jelly.

5  Break up the chocolate and put with cream in a bowl over a pan of hot water. Stir until it is smooth. Spread the cake with the icing. Serve with cream (optional).

# Queen Fabiola cake

## Ingredients

For the mixture:
*275g/10oz/10oz margarine*
*275g/10oz/10oz castor sugar*
*(fine granulated)*
*1x5ml/1tsp/1tsp vanilla essence*
*(extract)*
*5 eggs*
*1 ½ egg whites*
*3 drops almond essence (extract)*
*1x5ml/1tsp/1tsp rum essence*
*(extract)*
*salt*
*275g/10oz/10oz plain flour (all*
*purpose)*
*75g/3oz/6tbs cornflour*
*(cornstarch)*
*2x5ml/2tsp/2tsp baking powder*
*100g/4oz/¾lb candied peel,*
*chopped*

For the icing (frosting):
*175g/6oz/6oz icing sugar*
*(confectioners)*
*½ egg white*
*3x15ml/3tbs/4tbs lemon juice*

Decoration:
*50g/2oz/4tbs angelica*

## Method

Preheat the oven to 180°C/350°F/Gas 4.
1   To make the mixture: Cream margarine until it is fluffy. Add sugar and vanilla and beat until the magarine and sugar are a foamy white mixture. Gradually beat in the eggs and egg whites, almond and rum essence and salt.
2   Mix together the flour, cornflour and baking powder. Sift and fold into the mixture. Add candied peel and pour into a greased cake ring (23cm/9'') and bake for 65-75 minutes.
3   To make the icing: Sieve the icing sugar and stir together with ½ egg white and lemon juice until it is a thick liquid mixture. Spread cooled cake with this icing.
    Cut the angelica into leaves and stalks to decorate the cake.

# Viennese shortcake

**Ingredients**

For the mixture:
*6 eggs*
*350g/12oz/³⁄₄lb castor sugar*
*(fine granulated)*
*2x5ml/2tsp/2tsp vanilla essence*
*(extract)*
*2x15ml/2tbs/3tbs water*
*175g/6oz/6oz plain flour*
*(all purpose)*
*175g/6oz/6oz cornflour*
*(cornstarch)*
*2x5ml/2tsp/2tsp baking powder*
*350g/12oz/³⁄₄lb melted butter*

For the apricot glaze:
*3x15ml/3tbs/4tbs apricot jam*
*(jelly)*
*3x15ml/3tbs/4tbs apricot*
*brandy*
*1x15ml/1tbs/1tbs water*

For the icing:
*25g/1oz/2tbs icing sugar*
*(confectioners)*
*½ egg white*

**Method**

Preheat oven to 160°C/325°F/Gas 3.
1   To make the mixture: Take half an egg white from the 6 eggs and keep separate and covered. Put the eggs into a bowl and beat together with the sugar and vanilla. Add the water.

2   Sift together the flour, cornflour, baking powder and fold into the egg mixture gradually. Carefully add the warm melted

butter. Pour mixture into a greased spiral pattern cake tin (23cm/9'') and bake for 60-85 minutes until needle comes out clean. Turn out on to a wire tray, leave to cool.

3   To make the apricot glaze: Sieve the apricot jam and stirring constantly bring to the boil with the apricot brandy and water. Spread the glaze over the shortcake.

4   To make the icing: Sieve the icing sugar and stir together with the reserved egg white. If necessary, add some water and keep stirring until it becomes a smooth mixture, thick enough to pipe.

5   Fill a conical greaseproof paper bag with the icing. Cut off the tip of the bag and use to pipe over the shortcake.

# Anna cake

## Ingredients

*225g/8oz/½lb butter or margarine*
*225g/8oz/½lb castor sugar (fine granulated)*
*1x5ml/1tsp/1tsp vanilla essence (extract)*
*4 eggs*
*1x5ml/1tsp/1tsp rum essence (extract)*
*225g/8oz/½lb plain flour (all purpose)*
*2x5ml/2tsp/2tsp baking powder*
*100g/4oz/¼lb plain chocolate, grated*
*100g/4oz/¼lb ground almonds*
*50g/2oz/4tbs candied peel, chopped*

Decoration: *icing sugar (confectioners)*

## Method

   Preheat oven to 180°C/350°F/Gas 4
1  Cream the butter until fluffy. Gradually beat in the sugar, vanilla, eggs and rum essence.

2  Sift together flour and baking powder. Fold into the butter mixture.

3  Sift together the chocolate, almonds and candied peel and stir into the mixture. Put the mixture into a greased, spring-release cake tin (23cm/9''). Do not grease the sides, and bake for about 60 minutes, until well risen and golden.

   To decorate - sift the cake with icing sugar.

# Juliana cake

## Ingredients

For the mixture:
*350g/12oz/³/₄lb butter or margarine*
*275g/10oz/10oz castor sugar*
*(fine granulated)*
*1x5ml/1tsp/1tsp vanilla essence*
*(extract)*
*4 eggs*
*2x15ml/2tbs/3tbs water*
*175g/6oz/6oz plain flour (all purpose)*
*2x5ml/2tsp/2tsp baking powder*
*175g/6oz/6oz ground hazelnuts*

For the icing (frosting) and decoration:
*150g/5oz/5oz plain chocolate*
*knob of butter*
*whipped cream and glacé*
*cherries*

## Method

Preheat oven to 180°C/350°F/Gas 4.
1  Cream the butter until fluffy. Gradually beat in the sugar, vanilla, eggs and water.
2  Sift together the flour and baking powder, fold into the butter mixture. Stir in the ground hazelnuts. Put the mixture into a greased ring tin (25cm/10''), dusted with ground hazelnuts. Bake for about 55 minutes until well risen.
3  To make the icing: break the chocolate into small pieces and stir with butter in a bowl over a pan of hot water until melted into a smooth mixture.
   Spread the chocolate icing over the cooled cake.
   Decorate the cake with whipped cream and glacé cherries.

*Juliana cake*

# Grilled layer cake

## Ingredients

For the icing (frosting):
*100g/4oz/¹/4lb chocolate*
*25g/1oz/2tbs butter*

For the mixture:
*225g/8oz/¹/2lb butter or margarine*
*225g/8oz/¹/2lb castor sugar (fine granulated)*
*1x5ml/1tsp/1tsp vanilla essence (extract)*
*6 eggs*
*2x15ml/2tbs/3tbs rum*
*150g/5oz/5oz plain flour (all purpose)*
*100g/4oz/¹/4lb cornflour (cornstarch)*
*3x5ml/3tsp/3tsp baking powder*

**Method:**

1 Separate the yolks and whites of the eggs. Cream the butter until fluffy. Gradually beat in the sugar, vanilla, 2 eggs, 4 egg yolks and rum.

2 Sift together the flour, cornflour, baking powder and fold into the butter mixture. Beat 4 egg whites until stiff. Carefully fold into the mixture.

3 Cover the base of a spring-release tin (23cm/9") with greased greaseproof paper. Take 1x15ml/1tbs/2tbs of the mixture and spread it evenly with a brush over the cake tin base. Put the tin on a grid under a preheated grill, leaving a distance of about 20cm/8" and bake the cake layer light brown, about 3 mins.

4 For the second layer, brush 1x15ml/1tbs/2tbs of the mixture over the grilled layer and put the tin back under the grill. Carry on in this way until all the mixture is finished, ensure that the distance between the grill and top of the cake is 20cm/8" as the cake increases in size.

5 When cake is baked, carefully loosen it with a knife around the edges of the tin. Turn the cake out on to a baking sheet, pull off the greaseproof paper and immediately put the cake into a hot oven (200°C/400°F/Gas 6) for 5 minutes.

6 To make the icing: Put the chocolate and butter into a bowl over a pan of hot water and stir until it is smooth. When the cake is cold spread it with the icing.

# Spice cake

## Ingredients

For the apricot glaze:
*3x15ml/3tbs/4tbs apricot jam*
*(jelly)*
*1x15ml/1tbs/2tbs water*

For the icing (frosting):
*75g/3oz/6tbs chocolate*
*3x15ml/3tbs/4tbs cream*

For the mixture:
*100g/4oz/¼lb honey*
*50g/2oz/4tbs castor sugar*
*(fine granulated)*
*1x5ml/1tsp/1tsp vanilla essence*
*(extract)*
*100g/4oz/¼lb butter or*
*margarine*

*2 eggs*
*pinch of ground cloves*
*pinch of ground cardamom*
*1x5ml/1tsp/1tsp ground cinnamon*
*grated rind of 1 orange*
*225g/8oz/½lb plain flour (all purpose)*
*3x5ml/3tsp/3tsp baking powder*
*2x15ml/2tbs/3tbs orange juice*
*50g/2oz/4tbs orange candied peel, chopped*
*50g/2oz/4tbs almonds, chopped*

## Method

Preheat oven to 180°C/350°C/Gas 4.

1 Slowly heat the honey, sugar, vanilla and butter or margarine until all the ingredients are melted. Pour into a mixing bowl and put in a cold place. Stir the eggs, cloves, cardamom, cinnamon and orange rind through the nearly cold mixture.

2 Sift together the baking powder and flour, and fold into the mixture. Add orange juice. Finally stir in the candied orange peel and almonds.

3 Put mixture into a greased, spring-release cake tin (23cm/9"). Spread it smoothly and bake for about 35 minutes.

4 To make the apricot glaze: Strain apricot jam and boil briefly with water. Spread the glaze on the cake while the cake is still warm. Leave to cool.

5 To make the icing: Break chocolate into pieces. Put it into a bowl over a pan of hot water until it is soft, then stir in the cream until it is a smooth mixture. Spread the cake with icing and decorate with the blanched almond halves.

# Chocolate log

## Ingredients

For the mixture:
*100g/4oz/¹/₄lb butter or
margarine
150g/5oz/5oz castor sugar
(fine granulated)
4 eggs
100g/4oz/¹/₄lb chocolate
50g/2oz/4tbs plain flour
(all purpose)
2 pkts chocolate blancmange
powder
2x5ml/2tsp/2tsp baking powder
75g/3oz/6tbs ground almonds
or ground hazelnuts*

For the icing (frosting):
*125g/5oz/5oz icing sugar
(confectioners)
25g/1oz/2tbs cocoa
1x15ml/1tbs/2tbs hot water
25g/1oz/2tbs butter*

Decoration: *40g/1 ¹/₂oz/3tbs
blanched almonds*

## Method

Preheat oven to 180°C/350°F/Gas 4.
1   To make the mixture: Cream the butter until fluffy, gradually
beat in sugar and eggs. Grate chocolate and add.
2   Sift together the flour, blancmange powder and baking powder.
Fold into the butter mixture. If necessary, add
2x15ml/2tbs/3tbs of milk (take care not to make the mixture
too runny).
3   Finally, fold the ground almonds or hazelnuts into the mixture.
Put the mixture into a greased Swiss roll tin (jelly roll tin) and
bake for 50-60 minutes, until well risen and firm.
4   To make the icing: Sift together the icing sugar and cocoa.
Pour in hot water and stir until the mixture is thick and
creamy. Melt butter and stir into the chocolate mixture and
spread over the cooled cake.

Stud the cake with sliced almonds.

# Contents

# Index